RACISM IN AMERICA AND BLACK MENTAL HEALTH

KATHERINE GROSSMAN; WALTER PALMER

authorHOUSE®

AuthorHouse™
1663 Liberty Drive
Bloomington, IN 47403
www.authorhouse.com
Phone: 833-262-8899

Published by AuthorHouse 08/25/2021

ISBN: 978-1-6655-3650-9 (sc)
ISBN: 978-1-6655-3655-4 (e)

Written by Katherine Grossman
for The W.D. Palmer Foundation
as directed by W.D. Palmer

Cover Art by Katherine Grossman

CONTENTS

WALTER D. PALMER LEADERSHIP SCHOOL

Currently W. D. Palmer is the founder and director of the W. D. Palmer Foundation (est. 1955), a repository of information-gathering on racism in health, education, employment, housing, courts, prisons, higher education, military, government, politics, law, banking, insurance, etc.

He is also the founder of the Black People's University of Philadelphia (1955) Freedom School, which was the grassroots organizing and training center for grassroots community and political leadership in Philadelphia and nationally. These organizations were run as nonprofit unincorporated associations from 1955 until 1980, when the Palmer Foundation received its 501(c)(3) federal tax exemption status.

W. D. Palmer has also been a professor, teaching American Racism at the University of Pennsylvania since the 1960's and today he is a member of the Presidents Commission on 1619, the 400-year anniversary of African slavery in America.

Professor Palmer has been a social activist leading the fight against racial injustice for over seventy years in Philadelphia and around the nation. In 2018, Philadelphia honored him for the organizing work he did to reform the Philadelphia school system in 1967.

In 2020, Philadelphia honored him for 65 years of fighting for social justice throughout the country. In 1980, he led the fight for parental school choice which helped the Governor of

Pennsylvania get a law passed in 1997, and in 2000 he created the Walter D. Palmer Leadership Charter School.

In 2005, he borrowed eleven million dollars to build a 55 thousand square-foot two story building on two acres of land in North Philadelphia, which was donated to the school by the City of Philadelphia, and because of the school's rapid growth, in 2010 he acquired the Saint Bartholomew Catholic High School, for his middle and high school.

In ten years, the school grew from three hundred elementary and middle school students, to two hundred preschoolers and over a thousand kindergarten to twelfth graders. In 2005,

W. D. Palmer commissioned a muralist to paint over four hundred pre-selected portraits on the school walls, corridors, and stairwells, with a goal to paint thirty fifteen foot murals in the gymnatorium.

Although the Walter D. Palmer Leadership School recruited "at risk children" that were from seventeen of the poorest zip codes in Philadelphia and 300 percent below poverty, the school boasted of a 95% daily attendance, 100% high school graduation, and 100% post graduate placement in four year and two year colleges, trade and technology schools, or military, until the school's closing in 2015.

ACKNOWLEDGEMENT

I would like to take this time to acknowledge from the beginning of the Palmer Foundation, 1955, the many contributors who helped to gather information, organize, and write the leadership, self-development, and social awareness curriculums.

From the Palmer Foundation's inception, these contributors have been composed of community members, elementary, middle- and high-school students, as well as college student volunteers and interns, along with professional contributors.

We chose this method and process because it was consistent with our history, vision, philosophy, mission, and goals of always developing leadership in practice.

These groups, who have helped to produce our materials, are the same cohorts who over the years have helped to teach and train others as well as helped to develop a national database through which these curriculum and training materials can be distributed.

The story of the Palmer Foundation is the story of building community and leadership at the same time, and the Palmer Foundation wants to give an enthusiastic endorsement in recognition of the thousands of people who have been with us on this long and arduous journey.

We want to take this time to thank the many community leaders and people that have invited us into their communities to help them reclaim and restore the many values, properties, and people who may have been threatened with the loss of finance, property, and life, because they are the true heroes and heroines that made the Palmer Foundation the success that it has become.

Public Appeal

The Palmer Foundation is a federal 501(c)(3) organization that has spent over 65 years educating and fighting for social justice in the most underserved "at risk" communities around the country. Our goals have always been to use education for human liberation and encourage "at risk" families and children to help gather, write, produce, publish, and teach others in a similar situation.

Our mission is to disseminate our leadership, self-development, social justice, and grassroots-organizing books, manuals, and learning materials across America and around the world.

Our goals are to sell these publications or to offer them in exchange for a suggested tax-exempt donation that would allow us to continue producing our leadership training, as well as grassroots community and political organizing efforts.

Ultimately, we would like to create a satellite school as a model or prototype of the Walter D. Palmer Leadership School that could be replicated around the world, and we appeal for your enthusiastic and sustained support going forward.

SYNOPSIS

From doctors' experimentation on slaves to the Black Lives Matter movement, mental healthcare for Black Americans requires an in-depth investigation into how we got to where we are today. *Racism in America: Black Mental Health* provides an overview of the historical and modern development of mental health among Black Americans. Issues such as the criminalization of mental health issues, distrust in healthcare systems, and the effects of racial discrimination are explored to offer insights into the future of Black mental health.

RESOURCES

If you or anyone you know are contemplating suicide, you can reach out to the National Suicide Prevention Lifeline, day or night, at 1-800-273-8255.

This publication provides an overview of Black mental health in the United States. It is not meant to act as a diagnostic resource.

INTRODUCTION

The historical oppression, dehumanization, and violence against Black bodies and minds in the United States has resulted in a healthcare system incapable of treating mental health in Black Americans. In addition to the racism still present today—structurally, systemically, and individually—there persists a racial trauma inflicted upon Black Americans, producing not only feelings of grief, isolation, and pain, but also a distrust of the healthcare system.

In 2019, suicide was the second leading cause of death for Black Americans ages 15 to 24.[1] A report from the U.S. Surgeon General found that from 1980 to 1995, the suicide rate among Black Americans ages 10 to 14 increased by 233%, as compared to 120% for non-Hispanic whites.[2] Black females, grades 9-12, were 60 percent more likely to attempt suicide in 2019 as compared to non-Hispanic white females of the same age.[3] In 2019, 19.8% of non-Hispanic White adults age 18 and over received mental health services in the past year, while only 9.8% of non-Hispanic Black adults did so.[4]

Attempting to explain and interpret these troubling statistics requires research not only into today's practices, but also the historical development of Black mental health. Limited access to mental health resources, poor treatment facilities, as well as the criminalization of mental health issues over the past two centuries has resulted in a healthcare system severely impacted by racism.

Due to institutionalized racism, Black Americans are disproportionately represented in the populations that experience homelessness, poverty, prison, and foster care, factors which can lead to heightened anxiety and depression. Black mental health cannot be separated from the efforts of activists to resist Jim Crow, participate in the Civil Rights Movement, or battle the War on Crime. Understanding these events and perspectives is necessary to providing competent care to Black Americans. Efforts for equitable housing, healthcare, employment, pay, safety, and suffrage are all efforts to improve Black mental health. However, the blame does not solely lie with

---

[1] U.S. Department of Health and Human Services Office of Minority Health. "Mental and Behavioral Health - African Americans." Mental and Behavioral Health - African Americans. Accessed March 25, 2021. https://minorityhealth.hhs.gov/omh/browse.aspx?lvl=4&lvlid=24.

[2] Ibid.

[3] Ibid.

[4] Ibid.

institutions. Personally mediated racism, as defined by C.P. Jones[5] as intentional or unintentional discriminatory acts against people of color through negative interpersonal interactions and prejudice, is another obstruction to improving Black mental health. Discrimination towards Black Americans results in psychological stress and is associated with an increased risk of Major Depressive Disorder.[6] Additionally, when MDD affects African Americans and Caribbean blacks, it is usually untreated and is more severe and disabling compared with that in non-Hispanic whites.[7]

Furthermore, patients seeking care continue to face discrimination. Black patients often face negative experiences in healthcare, misdiagnosing, and differential treatment. Rheeda Walker, the author of *The Unapologetic Guide to Black Mental Health*, writes that "for those who say that the problem is classism and poverty, I tell you that a lot of disparities in health exist even after researchers adjust for income and whether or not someone has health insurance."[8]

[5] Jones, Camara Phyllis. 2000. "Levels of Racism: A Theoretic Framework and a Gardener's Tale." *American Journal of Public Health* 90 (8): 1212–15. https://doi.org/10.2105/AJPH.90.8.1212.

[6] Williams, David R., and Selina A. Mohammed. 2009. "Discrimination and Racial Disparities in Health: Evidence and Needed Research." *Journal of Behavioral Medicine* 32 (1): 20–47. https://doi.org/10.1007/s10865-008-9185-0.

[7] Williams, David R., Hector M. González, Harold Neighbors, Randolph Nesse, Jamie M. Abelson, Julie Sweetman, and James S. Jackson. 2007. "Prevalence and Distribution of Major Depressive Disorder in African Americans, Caribbean Blacks, and Non-Hispanic Whites: Results From the National Survey of American Life." *Archives of General Psychiatry* 64 (3): 305. https://doi.org/10.1001/archpsyc.64.3.305.

[8] Walker, Rheeda. 2020. *The Unapologetic Guide to Black Mental Health: Navigate an Unequal System, Learn Tools for Emotional Wellness, and Get the Help You Deserve.* New Harbinger Publications, Inc.

AN HISTORICAL OVERVIEW

Understanding the history of Black bodies and minds is imperative to understanding the state of Black mental health in America today. The common connection between Black people and the early healthcare system was violence. Doctors and psychologists have reinforced racism at every level of their practices. Slaves were experimented upon to attempt to find solutions to physical and mental problems for white people. Reviewing the history of the role of Black Americans in the healthcare system reveals clearly why there are reduced levels of trust among Black Americans in research.

Notoriously, the physician Samuel A. Cartwright created the "mental illnesses" of drapetomonia (the disease that caused slaves to run away), rascality (the disease that made slaves commit petty offenses), and dysaesthesia ethiopica (the disease that made slaves insensible and indifferent to punishment). Cartwright's use of race is not uncommon in the national healthcare system which attempts to highlight the perceived internal and anatomical differences between Black and white bodies.[9]

Doctors believing in biological differences between races still has effects today. Doctors believe Black people have higher pain tolerance that white people, which causes misdiagnosing of illnesses and unequal recommendations for treatment.[10] Additionally, racism in medical standards and practices is used as a tool in white supremacy. In 1968, the American Psychological Association changed the definition of schizophrenia to include "aggression," targeting those who participated in civil rights activism.

This is only one of many reasons why Black people are reluctant to seek out care for mental health issues. The most notorious example of harm done by the healthcare system is the Tuskegee Study, which aimed to research syphilis in 600 Black men. Beginning in 1932 and ran by the Public Health Service and Tuskegee Institute, the Tuskegee Study was conducted without the patients' informed consent and the subjects were never given the choice to quit the study. Even

---

[9] Willoughby, Christopher. 2018. "Running Away from Drapetomania: Samuel A. Cartwright, Medicine, and Race in the Antebellum South." *The Journal of Southern History* 84 (3): 579–614.

[10] Williams, David R., and Selina A. Mohammed. 2009. "Discrimination and Racial Disparities in Health: Evidence and Needed Research." *Journal of Behavioral Medicine* 32 (1): 20–47. https://doi.org/10.1007/s10865-008-9185-0.

when the highly effective penicillin became the drug of choice to treat syphilis in 1947, it was not offered to the subjects by the researchers. One study found that knowledge of the Tuskegee Study resulted in less trust of researchers and a lower likelihood to participate in research studies, particularly among Black Americans.[11]

---

[11] Shavers, Vickie L, Charles F Lynch, and Leon F Burmeister. 2000. "Knowledge of the Tuskegee study and its impact on the willingness to participate in medical research studies." *Journal of the National Medical Association* 92 (12): 10.

CRIMINALIZATION OF BLACK COMMUNITIES

The criminalization of mental health issues affects everyone who is afflicted with mental illness, not just Black Americans. As policy began to favor deinstitutionalization, the responsibility to manage those with mental health issues shifted from mental health institutions to the police and courts, racist institutions that disproportionally harm Black Americans. Of those who come into the juvenile justice system, Black youth are more likely to be placed in a juvenile facility or transferred to and sentenced by an adult criminal court, while white youth are much more likely to be placed on probation or placed in a diversion program where they can receive mental health services.[12]

Drug crimes also disproportionally harm Black Americans. Concern from parents and an emerging crack cocaine epidemic created a public movement against drug use in the 1980s that contributed to the drastic rise in incarceration rates. As crack cocaine appeared in Black and Latino communities, the media reinforced racial stereotypes by telling stories about "crack whores," "crack babies," and "gangbangers" selling the drug.

In 1981, shortly after Ronald Reagan took office, his wife, Nancy, began a highly- publicized anti-drug campaign, popularizing the phrase "Just Say No." In Reagan's War on Drugs campaign, greater federal funding was given to the FBI and the Department of Defense in order to crack down on drugs. The Anti-Drug Abuse Act of 1986 allowed public housing authorities to evict tenants with any drug-related criminal activity and eliminated federal benefits, including student loans, for those with drug offenses. It also established a 100-to-1 crack versus powder cocaine sentencing disparity under which distribution of only five grams of crack cocaine results in a minimum 5-year federal prison sentence, while distribution of five hundred grams of powder cocaine carries the same 5-year mandatory minimum sentence.

As the crack epidemic began to decline in the late 1980s, the federal government focused its drug policies elsewhere, particularly on marijuana. This enforcement especially negatively impacted low-income Black communities. Bill Clinton was one of the greatest advocates for tough crime policies and continued to escalate the drug war. He supported Three Strikes legislation

---

[12] Redfield, Sarah E., and Jason P. Nance. 2016. "American Bar Association: Joint Task Force on Reversing the School-to-Prison Pipeline." *University of Memphis Law Review* 47 (1): 1–180.

and created a "One Strike, You're Out" initiative that evicted many minorities from housing. In addition, one could not receive welfare assistance if convicted of a felony drug offense. Famously, Clinton rejected a U.S. Sentencing Commission recommendation that would eliminate the disparity between crack and powder cocaine sentences. The Clinton Administrations "tough-on-crime" policies resulted in the largest increases in federal and state prison inmates of any president in American history.

Even with public opinion surrounding marijuana use becoming more progressive, the racial disparity for marijuana possession remains. On average, a Black person is 3.6 times more likely to be arrested for marijuana possession than a white person, despite the fact that Black and white people use marijuana at similar rates.[13] In the states with the worst disparities, Black people were on average over nine times more likely than white people to be arrested for marijuana possession.[14]

---

[13] American Civil Liberties Union. 2020. "A Tale of Two Countries: Racially Targeted Arrests in the Era of Marijuana Reform." American Civil Liberties Union. https://www.aclu.org/report/tale-two-countries-racially-targeted-arrests-era-marijuana-reform.

[14] Ibid.

RACIAL TRAUMA AND DISCRIMINATION

The recent surge of Black deaths at the hands of law enforcement officials has a lasting and profound effect on individual and collective Black mental health. Bor et al. finds that each additional police killing of an unarmed Black American was associated with 0.14 additional poor mental health days among Black American respondents, with effects lasting 1–2 months after exposure.[15] In addition to criminal justice and police reform to decrease these events, the resulting adverse mental health affects within communities should be mitigated.

Current events are not the only thing affecting mental health exclusively among Black Americans. Joy Degruy describes Post Traumatic Slave Syndrome as the residual impacts of generations of slavery on Black mental health.[16] Jameta Nicole Barlow also explores intergenerational

[15] Bor, Jacob, Atheendar S Venkataramani, David R Williams, and Alexander C Tsai. 2018. "Police Killings and Their Spillover Effects on the Mental Health of Black Americans: A Population-Based, Quasi-Experimental Study." *The Lancet* 392 (10144): 302–10. https://doi.org/10.1016/S0140-6736(18)31130-9.

[16] Degruy-Leary, Joy. *Post-traumatic Slave Syndrome: America's legacy of enduring injury.* Portland, OR: Joy DeGruy Publications Inc, 2017.

gendered racialized trauma—"the legacy of trauma within, among, and throughout generations of Black women, uniquely influenced by the construction of gender and race in the United States and consequential intersectional experiences and associated lifestyle comorbidities, all a direct result of colonialism."[17]

Mental health professionals, especially those who interact with Black youth, are often unprepared or unqualified to address race's impact on mental health. For example, when there is an act of violence in a school in a white community, mental health professionals are immediately called in to evaluate and address the needs of students. In contrast, Black children who witness comparable violence personally or through media are generally not given access to such assistance from mental health professionals, despite the fact that untreated trauma-related symptoms increase their risk of later coming into contact with the criminal justice system.

Another topic affecting the state of mental health in Black Americans that is not properly treated for is everyday racial discrimination. Research finds that the "the psychosocial stress resulting from repeated and cumulative incidents of unfair treatment can trigger a host of emotional and cognitive responses (e.g., negative affect, sadness, rumination), which can heighten risk of psychopathology, including onset of depression."[18]

---

[17] Barlow, Jameta Nicole. 2018. "Restoring Optimal Black Mental Health and Reversing Intergenerational Trauma in an Era of Black Lives Matter." *Biography* 41 (4): 895–908. http://dx.doi.org.proxy.library.upenn.edu/10.1353/bio.2018.0084.

[18] Molina, Kristine M., and Drexler James. 2016. "Discrimination, Internalized Racism, and Depression: A Comparative Study of African American and Afro-Caribbean Adults in the US." *Group Processes & Intergroup Relations* 19 (4): 439–61. https://doi.org/10.1177/1368430216641304.

UNEQUAL TREATMENT

Discrimination continues to affect Black Americans when they do gain access to healthcare, whether for physical or mental health reasons. The same discrimination Black Americans face in their everyday lives is still present among healthcare professionals and can negatively affect Black Americans' experiences in accessing treatment. In an experiment to test racial bias in the mental health field, Shin et al. (2016) called counselors and psychologists using both a stereotypically Black-sounding names or a non–Latino White-sounding name. The caller with the stereotypically White-sounding name received voice messages that promoted the potential for services at a 12% higher rate than the caller with the stereotypically Black-sounding name.[19]

Unequal treatment in healthcare is not new to Black people. Even after the Civil Rights Act of 1964 was passed, mental health facilities in the South (particularly Mississippi and Alabama) remained segregated. A belief among doctors and nurses that Black people are able to withstand more pain than white people leads to undertreatment and misdiagnosing.[20] One study found that racial and ethnic minorities consistently receive less adequate treatment for acute and chronic pain than non-Hispanic whites, even after controlling for age, gender, and pain intensity.[21] Physicians are unaware of their own cultural beliefs and the role that stereotypes and biases play in the assessment and treatment of pain, even while underreporting pain intensity.

---

[19] Shin, Richard Q., Lance C. Smith, Jamie C. Welch, and Ijeoma Ezeofor. 2016. "Is Allison More Likely Than Lakisha to Receive a Callback From Counseling Professionals? A Racism Audit Study." *The Counseling Psychologist* 44 (8): 1187–1211. https://doi.org/10.1177/0011000016668814.

[20] Hoffman, Kelly M., Sophie Trawalter, Jordan R. Axt, and M. Norman Oliver. 2016. "Racial Bias in Pain Assessment and Treatment Recommendations, and False Beliefs about Biological Differences between Blacks and Whites." *Proceedings of the National Academy of Sciences of the United States of America* 113 (16): 4296–4301. https://doi.org/10.1073/pnas.1516047113.

[21] Mossey, Jana M. 2011. "Defining Racial and Ethnic Disparities in Pain Management." *Clinical Orthopaedics and Related Research* 469 (7): 1859–70. https://doi.org/10.1007/s11999-011-1770-9.

THE WAY FORWARD

Research suggests that increasing the diversity of mental health professionals would be helpful in improving care for Black Americans. Only 6.2% of psychologists, 5.6% of advanced-practice psychiatric nurses, 12.6% of social workers, and 21.3% of psychiatrists are members of minority groups.[22] Increasing the cultural competency of existing mental health professionals would reduce the effects of discrimination within healthcare access and treatment.

Social movements focusing on mental health in general and on the intersection of race and mental health have gained momentum in recent years. Social media and increased telehealth availability have become tools to provide greater access to Black Americans who seek mental health resources. Organizations such as the Black Mental Health Alliance and the Community Healing Network center the Black experience in their efforts to address mental health issues. However, a more intentional effort is needed in the general mental health field to research and address racial disparities.

---

[22] Black Mental Health Alliance. 2021. "Black Mental Health Alliance." 2021. https://blackmentalhealth.com/.

The passing of H.R.5469, the Pursuing Equity in Mental Health Act, in September 2020 is a step in the right direction. The Act establishes programs to support school-based mental health services and address racial and ethnic mental health disparities, including funding grants for mental health services that are trauma-informed and designed to provide comprehensive, culturally appropriate interventions at a school-wide level.

BIBLIOGRAPHY

Barlow, J. N. (2018). Restoring Optimal Black Mental Health and Reversing Intergenerational Trauma in an Era of Black Lives Matter. *Biography, 41*(4), 895–908. http://dx.doi.org.proxy.library.upenn.edu/10.1353/bio.2018.0084

Bor, J., Venkataramani, A. S., Williams, D. R., & Tsai, A. C. (2018). Police killings and their spillover effects on the mental health of black Americans: A population-based, quasi-experimental study. *The Lancet, 392*(10144), 302–310. https://doi.org/10.1016/S0140-6736(18)31130-9

Braunstein, J. B., Sherber, N. S., Schulman, S. P., Ding, E. L., & Powe, N. R. (2008). Race, Medical Researcher Distrust, Perceived Harm, and Willingness to Participate in Cardiovascular Prevention Trials. *Medicine, 87*(1), 1–9. https://doi.org/10.1097/MD.0b013e3181625d78

Gara, M. A., Minsky, S., Silverstein, S. M., Miskimen, T., & Strakowski, S. M. (2019). A Naturalistic Study of Racial Disparities in Diagnoses at an Outpatient Behavioral Health Clinic. *Psychiatric Services, 70*(2), 130–134. https://doi.org/10.1176/appi.ps.201800223

Goff, P. A., Eberhardt, J. L., Williams, M. J., & Jackson, M. C. (2008). Not yet human: Implicit knowledge, historical dehumanization, and contemporary consequences. *Journal of Personality and Social Psychology, 94*(2), 292–306. https://doi.org/10.1037/0022-3514.94.2.292

Griffith, E. E. H., Jones, B. E., & Stewart, A. J. (2018). *Black Mental Health: Patients, Providers, and Systems*. American Psychiatric Association Publishing. http://ebookcentral.proquest.com/lib/upenn-ebooks/detail.action?docID=5524374

Grills, C. N., Aird, E. G., & Rowe, D. (2016). Breathe, Baby, Breathe: Clearing the Way for the Emotional Emancipation of Black People. *Cultural Studies ↔ Critical Methodologies, 16*(3), 333–343. https://doi.org/10.1177/1532708616634839

Hoffman, K. M., Trawalter, S., Axt, J. R., & Oliver, M. N. (2016). Racial bias in pain assessment and treatment recommendations, and false beliefs about biological differences between blacks and whites. *Proceedings of the National Academy of Sciences of the United States of America, 113*(16), 4296–4301. https://doi.org/10.1073/pnas.1516047113

Hoge, M. A., Stuart, G. W., Morris, J., Flaherty, M. T., Paris, M., & Goplerud, E. (2013). Mental Health And Addiction Workforce Development: Federal Leadership Is Needed To

Address The Growing Crisis. *Health Affairs*, *32*(11), 2005–2012. https://doi.org/10.1377/hlthaff.2013.0541

Katz, A. D., & Hoyt, W. T. (20140317). The influence of multicultural counseling competence and anti-Black prejudice on therapists' outcome expectancies. *Journal of Counseling Psychology*, *61*(2), 299. https://doi.org/10.1037/a0036134

Kirwan Institute for the Study of Race and Ethnicity. (2017). *State of the Science: Implicit Bias Review*. Kirwan Institute for the Study of Race and Ethnicity. http://kirwaninstitute.osu.edu/implicit-bias-training/resources/2017-implicit-bias-review.pdf Molina, K. M., & James, D. (2016). Discrimination, internalized racism, and depression: A comparative study of African American and Afro-Caribbean adults in the US. *Group Processes & Intergroup Relations*, *19*(4), 439–461. https://doi.org/10.1177/1368430216641304

Mossey, J. M. (2011). Defining Racial and Ethnic Disparities in Pain Management. *Clinical Orthopaedics and Related Research*, *469*(7), 1859–1870. https://doi.org/10.1007/s11999-011-1770-9

Myers, L. J. (1993). *Understanding an Afrocentric world view: Introduction to an optimal psychology*. Kendall/Hunt Pub. Co. Paradies, Y., Ben, J., Denson, N., Elias, A., Priest, N., Pieterse, A., Gupta, A.,

Kelaher, M., & Gee, G. (2015). Racism as a Determinant of Health: A Systematic Review and Meta-Analysis. *PLoS ONE*, *10*(9). https://doi.org/10.1371/journal.pone.0138511

Parham, T. A., White, J. L., Ajamu, A., & White, J. L. (2000). *The psychology of Blacks: An African-centered perspective* (3rd ed). Prentice Hall.

Pieterse, A. L., Todd, N. R., Neville, H. A., & Carter, R. T. (2012). Perceived racism and mental health among Black American adults: A meta-analytic review. *Journal of Counseling Psychology*, *59*(1), 1–9. https://doi.org/10.1037/a0026208

Rogowski, J. C., & Cohen, C. J. (n.d.). *BLACK MILLENNIALS IN AMERICA*. 88.

Schulz, A. J., Gravlee, C. C., Williams, D. R., Israel, B. A., Mentz, G., & Rowe, Z. (2006). Discrimination, Symptoms of Depression, and Self-Rated Health Among African American Women in Detroit: Results From a Longitudinal Analysis. *American Journal of Public Health*, *96*(7), 1265–1270. https://doi.org/10.2105/AJPH.2005.064543

Shavers, V. L., Lynch, C. F., & Burmeister, L. F. (2000). Knowledge of the Tuskegee Study and its Impact on the Willingness to Participate in Medical Research Studies. *Journal of the National Medical Association*, *92*(12), 10.

Shin, R. Q., Smith, L. C., Welch, J. C., & Ezeofor, I. (2016). Is Allison More Likely Than Lakisha to Receive a Callback From Counseling Professionals? A Racism Audit Study. *The Counseling Psychologist*, *44*(8), 1187–1211. https://doi.org/10.1177/0011000016668814

Speight, S. L. (2007). Internalized Racism: One More Piece of the Puzzle. *The Counseling Psychologist, 35*(1), 126–134. https://doi.org/10.1177/0011000006295119

U.S. Department of Health and Human Services Office of Minority Health. (n.d.). *Mental and Behavioral Health—African Americans.* Mental and Behavioral Health - African Americans. Retrieved March 25, 2021, from https://minorityhealth.hhs.gov/omh/browse.aspx?lvl=4&lvlid=24

Walker, R. (2020). *The unapologetic guide to Black mental health: Navigate an unequal system, learn tools for emotional wellness, and get the help you deserve.* New Harbinger Publications, Inc.

Washington, H. A. (2006). *Medical apartheid: The dark history of medical experimentation on Black Americans from colonial times to the present* (1st ed). Doubleday.

Williams, D. R., González, H. M., Neighbors, H., Nesse, R., Abelson, J. M.,

Sweetman, J., & Jackson, J. S. (2007). Prevalence and Distribution of Major Depressive Disorder in African Americans, Caribbean Blacks, and Non-Hispanic Whites: Results From the National Survey of American Life. *Archives of General Psychiatry, 64*(3), 305. https://doi.org/10.1001/archpsyc.64.3.305

Williams, D. R., & Mohammed, S. A. (2009). Discrimination and racial disparities in health: Evidence and needed research. *Journal of Behavioral Medicine, 32*(1), 20–47. https://doi.org/10.1007/s10865-008-9185-0

A Brief Biography of Professor Walter Palmer

After a tumultuous juvenile life, Professor Palmer graduated from high school and was hired by the University of Pennsylvania hospital as a surgical attendant and eventually was recruited into the University of Pennsylvania School of Inhalation and Respiratory (Oxygen) Therapy.

After his certification as an inhalation and respiratory therapist, he was hired by the Children's Hospital of Philadelphia as the Director of the Department of Inhalation and Respiratory (Oxygen) Therapy, where he spent ten years helping to develop the national field of cardio-pulmonary therapy.

In 1955, Professor Palmer created the Palmer Foundation and the Black People's University of Philadelphia Freedom School and would spend the next seventy years developing leaders for social justice nationally.

Professor Palmer has also pursued further education at Temple University for Business Administration and Communications, Cheyney State University for a Teacher's Degree in History and Secondary Education. And at age 40, acquired his juris doctorate in law from Howard University.

Between 1965 and 1995, he produced and hosted radio programs on Philadelphia WDAS, Atlantic City WUSS, and WFPG Radio, in addition to Philadelphia NBC TV 10 and New Jersey Suburban Cable Television.

In 2006, he was inducted into the Philadelphia College of Physicians as a Fellow for the body of work he had done over the past 70 years, after having spent ten (1980-1990) years as a licensed financial officer teaching poor people how to overcome poverty by saving and investing three dollars per day.

During that entire period, Professor Palmer led the Civil Rights, Black Power and Afrocentric movements in Philadelphia, around the country as well as the Caribbean and West Indies.

In the 1980s to 2015, he led the school choice movement, organized a state-wide parental school choice group which collected 500,000 petitions in 1997, which were used to create a charter and cyber school law in Pennsylvania, and in 2000 the Walter D. Palmer School was named after him.

In 1962, he created a school without walls on the University of Pennsylvania's campus and became a visiting lecturer in the Schools of Medicine, Law, Education, Wharton, History, Africana Studies, Engineering, and he currently is a lecturer in the Schools of Medicine, Social Work, and Urban Studies, where he teaches courses on American racism.

In 1969, he helped the University of Pennsylvania Graduate School of Social Work students and faculty create required courses on American racism, making the University of Pennsylvania the first school in American academia to have such courses.

In 2019, Professor Palmer was appointed to the President's Commission on commemorating the four hundred year (1619) anniversary of American slavery.

Over his many years of teaching, he has received the title of Teacher Par Excellence and has amassed over 1,000 medals, trophies, plaques, certificates, and awards for participation in multiple disciplines.

W. D. Palmer Foundation Hashtags

- #racedialogueusa
- #racismdialogueusa
- #atriskchildrenusa
- #youthorganizingusa
- #stopblackonblackusa
- #newleadershipusa
- #1619commemorationusa
- #africanslaveryusa
- #indigenouspeopleusa
- #afrocentricusa
- #civillibertiesusa
- #civilrightsusa
- #humanrightsusa
- #saveourchildrenusa
- #parentalschoolchoiceusa
- #wearyourmaskusa
- #defeatcovid19usa
- #socialdistanceusa

W.D. Palmer Foundation Publications

The Palmer Foundation was founded in 1955 and is a 501(c)3 tax-exempt organization that has spent over 65 years developing educational curriculum and learning materials for at-risk children, their parents, mentors, and teachers across the country.

We work with children from pre-school to high school with a focus on leadership, self-development, and social awareness.

Community Survivalist

Community Activist

International Activist

Human Rights Advocate

Contact Us
The W.D. Palmer Foundation (1955)
P.O. Box 22692
Philadelphia, PA 19110
(267) 738-1588
thewdpalmerfoundation@gmail.com
www.thewdpalmerfoundation.org
www.speakerservices.com

Donate to the
W.D. Palmer Foundation

Make a donation (purchase), from the W.D. Palmer Foundation, a 501(c)3 tax-exempt organization that has worked for over 65 years to educate urban and rural "at-risk" children and their families, since 1955.

We have developed and published education curriculum and learning materials on leadership, self-development, and social awareness and how to overcome illiteracy, poverty, crime, and racism for urban and rural at-risk children and their families.

You will get a bulk discount for fifty (50) books or more, and the larger the order, the greater the discount. If you need less than fifty books, please order them directly from the publisher using the information below.

Order from us:
The W.D. Palmer Foundation
P.O. Box 22692
Philadelphia, PA 19110
www.thewdpalmerfoundation.org
wdpalmer@gmail.com
(267) 738-1588

Order from our publisher:
Author House
1663 Liberty Drive
Bloomington, IN 47403
www.authorhouse.com
(833) 262-8899

Part-time income
The W.D. Palmer Foundation is looking for community members and students that would like to earn extra income as independent sales representatives. Contact us to learn more.

Race and Racism

All Ebooks are $3.99+

Everything You Must Know Before Race and Racism Dialogue

A precursor, dialogue, and debate about race and racism in America.

Where American Presidents Stood on Race and Racism in America

What position did each of the US presidents take on race and racism in America?

The W.D. Palmer Foundation
thewdpalmerfoundation@gmail.com thewdpalmerfoundation.org

Race and Racism

All Ebooks are $3.99+

Racism in American Stage and Screen

How American stage and movies fostered racism in America and around the world.

Racism in America and Black Mental Health

How Black people were affected mentally by race and racism in America.

The W.D. Palmer Foundation
thewdpalmerfoundation@gmail.com thewdpalmerfoundation.org

History

All Ebooks are $3.99+

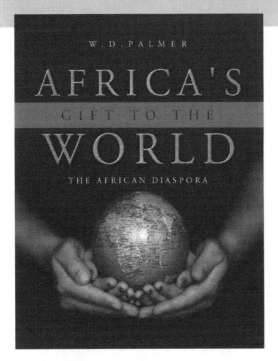

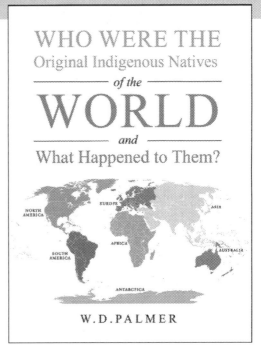

Africa's Gift to the World: The African Diaspora

How African humanity, culture, civilization, and history were spread all over the world through slavery.

Who were the Original Indigenous Natives of the World?

An attempt to answer questions of where people came from and where they went.

The W.D. Palmer Foundation
thewdpalmerfoundation@gmail.com thewdpalmerfoundation.org

Race, Racism, and Entertainment

All Ebooks are $3.99+

The Atlantic City Club Harlem

The story of how a nightclub was used to break down race and racism barriers in a small town.

MADD About Freedom

Major contributors in Music, Art, Dance, and Drama who used their talents for freedom.

The W.D. Palmer Foundation
thewdpalmerfoundation@gmail.com thewdpalmerfoundation.org

Leadership

All Ebooks are $3.99+

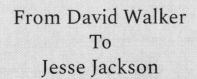

From David Walker To Jesse Jackson

David Walker
September 28 1796 - August 6, 1830

Jesse Jackson
October 8, 1941 - Present

Hollering for Freedom!

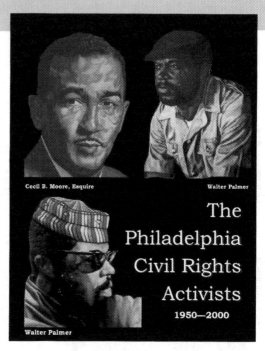

Cecil B. Moore, Esquire

Walter Palmer

The Philadelphia Civil Rights Activists
1950—2000

Walter Palmer

From David Walker to Jesse Jackson

Some of the most vocal people who spoke out for freedom.

Philadelphia Civil Rights Activists: 1950-2000

How two men helped shape the history and destiny of a major metropolitan city.

The W.D. Palmer Foundation
thewdpalmerfoundation@gmail.com thewdpalmerfoundation.org

Youth Advocacy

All Ebooks are $3.99+

Volume I

Appeal to all elementary, middle, high school, and college students and their parents to join the fight for social change!

Adopt an elementary, middle, high school, or college student, class, or school, or a church, for them to receive this survival guide

Volume I:
Alcohol Abuse
Animal Abuse
Asbestos
Bullying
Child Abuse
Disability
Disability Discrimination
Domestic Abuse
Drug Abuse
Education Discrimination

Volume II:
Elder Abuse
Employment Discrimination
Environmental Abuse
Ethnic Discrimination
Fighting
Fire Safety
Gambling Abuse
Gangs
Gender Discrimination
COVID-19

Volume III:
Gun Violence
Hate Crimes
HIV/AIDS
Homelessness
Housing Discrimination
Human Trafficking
Hunger
Labor Trafficking
Lead Poisoning
LGBT Discrimination

Volume IV:
Mental Health
Nutrition
Obesity
Pedophilia
Poison
Police Abuse
Public Accom. Discrim.
Racial Discrimination
Religious Discrimination
Runaways

Volume V:
School Dropout
Sex Trafficking
Sexual Assault
Sexual Harassment
Special Education
STDS
Stealing
Suicide
Teen Pregnancy
Water Safety

Professor W.D. Palmer and Age of Justice

A real-life comic hero appeal to parents, teachers, ministers, coaches, mentors, and monitors on how to help elementary, middle, high school, and first-year college students on where to turn in the face of danger.

The W.D. Palmer Foundation
thewdpalmerfoundation@gmail.com thewdpalmerfoundation.org

Youth Advocacy

All Ebooks are $3.99+

Professor W.D. Palmer and Age of Justice: Five-Volume Compendium

A collection of all five Age of Justice comic books into one volume.

The W.D. Palmer Foundation
thewdpalmerfoundation@gmail.com thewdpalmerfoundation.org

World Leaders

All Ebooks are $3.99+

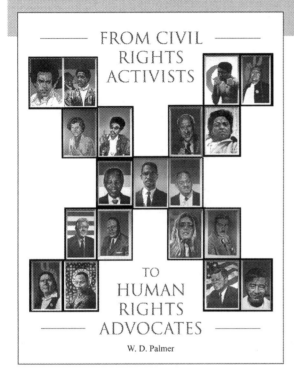

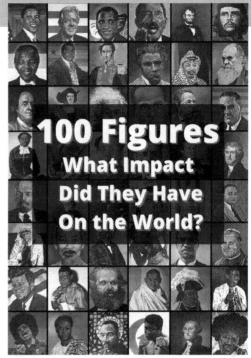

From Civil Rights Activists to Human Rights Advocates

How the fight for civil rights transformed activists into human rights advocates.

100 Figures

In what ways did 100 individuals impact the world?

Printed in the United States
by Baker & Taylor Publisher Services